365 DAYS

★★★★★★★★ OF ★★★★★★★★

MINDFULNESS

Yvette Jane

summersdale

365 DAYS OF MINDFULNESS

Copyright © Summersdale Publishers Ltd, 2012

Summersdale Publishers Ltd
46 West Street
Chichester
West Sussex
PO19 1RP
UK

www.summersdale.com

Printed and bound in the Czech Republic

ISBN: 978-1-84953-329-4

Substantial discounts on bulk quantities of Summersdale books are available to corporations, professional associations and other organisations. For details contact Nicky Douglas by telephone: +44 (0) 1243 756902, fax: +44 (0) 1243 786300 or email: nicky@summersdale.com.

To Alisha

with love and
peace
From charlotte x

INTRODUCTION

Mindfulness is about being aware of the present moment, without judgement or worry for the past or the future, calmly and peacefully. It allows you to experience the magic and wonder in this life that we have, and to listen to the wisdom of your own heart.

JANUARY

New Year's Day: Start a journal for this year in which you note down feelings, events and important conversations. It can sometimes help to make sense of things.

 Sort out old clothes – take them to a charity shop and visualise an updated, decluttered you for the new year.

 An affirmation is a quiet reminder repeated to yourself as you go about your day; let today's affirmation be 'relax'.

JANUARY

 On waking, spend some moments becoming aware of your body, listening to the sounds around you and noticing what thoughts are in your mind.

 While eating your meal, focus all your attention on eating, placing your fork down in between mouthfuls to take time while chewing. Savour each mouthful and bring awareness to every taste.

 When was the last time you did something for the first time? You are instinctively being mindful when your brain is engaged in something unfamiliar.

Plan to reduce the number of meetings you have at work, and set aside blocks of time without interruptions. This means you are not rushing from one meeting to the next.

 Place water outside for the birds – and stop to watch them wash and preen their feathers.

 If something difficult happens today, notice which parts of your body feel tense, then breathe into the area to help you relax.

Do less – do it more slowly, more fully and with more concentration.

 Visit a crystal shop and choose a small crystal to keep in your pocket. Hold it in your hand whenever you wish to feel calm and centred.

 At bedtime, sit for a moment to take stock of your day and review how you are feeling. Acknowledge this, and remind yourself 'all is well'.

I took a deep breath and listened to the old brag of my heart: I am, I am, I am.

Sylvia Plath

Until you make peace
with who you are, you'll
never be content with
what you have.

Doris Mortman

15 We all dash from one place to another – slow down with mindful walking. Take slower breaths, watch your feet as you place them on the ground, and bring awareness to your body as it moves.

 16 The next time it snows, stop to turn your face towards the sky and marvel at the beauty of snowflakes.

 17 Light a candle and reflect on how it brings illumination to the darkness, just as you can radiate brightly today in all you do.

As you drive or take a bus or train today, become aware of how you are sitting – relax your shoulders and head, unclench your hands, stretch your back and neck, and slow your breathing down.

 Try any kind of dance class this month where you can enjoy the music and be aware of every fibre in your body as you move. Have fun!

 Close your eyes and listen mindfully for one minute today to all the sounds around you. For one minute, you have nothing else to do. Just listen.

21 Dark winter evenings offer you the chance to reflect on your personal growth; old habits you wish to shift over winter and new projects to be birthed in spring.

 22 Take a moment today to focus on your breathing. It relaxes the space inside of you, straightens your spine, opens the chest and expands your heart.

 23 Place little notes around home and work to act as prompts for you to 'breathe', 'remember' and 'be mindful'.

Our minds are full of self-judgement, providing a constant noisy soundtrack in our heads. Be aware of this and of how it may be limiting today's decisions.

 First thing this morning, streamline your workday by taking a moment to set your priorities and make a short to-do list.

 Notice how you feel while watching a television programme. Become more conscious of what you choose to watch.

That's the way things come clear. All of a sudden. And then you realise how obvious they've been all along.

Madeleine L'Engle

Knowledge is learning something every day. Wisdom is letting go of something every day.

Zen proverb

29 Remember that sitting down to meditate is a big helping of mindfulness all in one go! Find out about classes today.

 30 If you usually avoid walking in the rain, don't! A walk in the rain can bring another dimension to your surroundings and there can be a heightened sense of smell, sound and feeling.

 31 Be especially aware of your judgements and expectations today. Let go of the stress of perfectionism.

FEBRUARY

1 Don't allow tension and stress to build up during the day. Stop, 'freeze'. Mentally scan your body for tension and make tiny adjustments to relax, or 'defrost'.

2 Say these words quietly to yourself throughout today: 'I am a being of peace.'

3 Find a few minutes in your morning routine to sit quietly and greet the day ahead, instead of rushing straight into your day's activities.

Make today a 'colour' day. Notice which colours you are drawn to. Become aware of colours in your workplace that you may not have noticed before.

 If sharing a family meal tonight, light a candle and place it on the table before you eat. This brings calm and peace to a setting, alleviates tension, and encourages everyone to eat more slowly and thoughtfully.

 Look into booking yourself a retreat weekend where you can take some time off to relax and focus on your wellbeing.

Plant hyacinth or daffodil bulbs in a pot and place by your computer or shelf at work. Observe each day as new life unfolds with the emerging spring.

 For a whole day, think and say positive things. Hold back on negative or sarcastic comments. Laugh at yourself when you discover how much negativity you carry in your mind.

 Whenever the phone rings today, use it as a reminder to stop, become aware of your breath and pick it up slowly to answer.

The secret of human freedom is to act well, without attachment to the results.

Bhagavad Gita

To live fully is to let go and die with each passing moment… to be reborn in each new one.

Jack Kornfield

Be mindful each time you wash your hands today. Pay close attention to the feel and temperature of the water on your skin and the scent of the soap.

 Join a laughter club or go with friends to some stand-up comedy. Sometimes we need to lighten up!

Valentine's Day: Say it with true meaning: 'I love you!'

 Imagine you are cultivating wisdom wherever you go and in whatever you do by being at peace.

If you are constantly rushing to appointments and other commitments, try giving yourself a more realistic timeframe. You'll arrive less stressed and more fully present.

 Today, accept things as they happen and accept people for who they are, including yourself.

 If there is ice on the windows this morning, stop for a moment to admire the intricate, fern-like patterns it forms and to appreciate the beauty of natural processes.

19 You have a choice in the way you react to things that annoy or upset you. Breathe slowly and deeply so that you can respond from a calm and centred place.

 20 Feel awareness through your feet – you are connected to Mother Earth with every step you take.

 21 Yoga and Pilates are great ways to connect mindfully with your body and your breath. Make plans today to check out a class.

Notice how children are delighted when it snows. Allow yourself to enjoy winter weather and take a moment to play, indoors or out.

 When you leave the house to shop today, move a little slower than usual. Enjoy the process without rushing and use all your senses at a leisurely pace.

 If you are feeling a little bleak this month, trust that new life follows on from winter. Take a walk and look for snowdrops and crocuses.

Never be afraid to sit awhile and think.

Lorraine Hansberry

For fast-acting relief, try slowing down.

Lily Tomlin

27 If something stresses you today, visualise it in a balloon, floating out of the window and into the clouds. Let it go.

 28 Place a photograph of nature or someone who makes you smile next to your computer. Look at it often and allow yourself to relax.

29

Leap Day: Pause and centre yourself before you leap into any decisions.

MARCH

⭐ **1** Before you begin any journey today, take a moment to centre yourself and set off with happiness and a sense of well-being.

⭐ **2** Don't miss an opportunity today to watch the wind gusting through the trees and whirling down the high street. Notice how nature touches everything.

⭐ **3** Make silence a part of your life today. Choose to make a conscious effort to switch off the noise around you, and allow the silence to fill your mind.

Allow yourself time to prepare and eat something different for breakfast with love and enjoyment, especially if you can share this with your family.

 Celebrate today's successes and achievements. Encourage and praise yourself before dashing on to new challenges.

 While doing housework, focus on what you are physically doing. Rather than rush through it as a 'chore', view it as a positive and loving commitment to your home completed with thorough care.

Focus on any object for one minute. Set thoughts and judgements to one side as you focus on the present time with mindfulness.

 Slow your driving down – keep to the speed limit and pay extra awareness to pedestrians and other road-users.

 Dance! Even if it is just in your front room, allow your mind to focus on the music and the movement of your body.

 The Sanskrit greeting 'namaste' means 'the light in me greets the light in you'; step back and fully see the people you interact with, not just as job titles or the clothes they wear.

Those who are always
preoccupied with
something cannot enjoy
the world.

Lao Tzu

Walking on water is
certainly miraculous,
but walking peacefully
on earth is an even
greater miracle.

John Gray

Take a moment to 'belly breathe' for a greater flow of oxygen and instant calm. Breathe in deeply, allowing your stomach to rise outwards. On the out breath, allow your stomach to fall back.

 Spend today without snacking on the run – if it's possible, sit down at a table to eat with mindfulness.

World Sleep Day (third Friday in March): Before you go to bed tonight, spend a minute breathing out the negative experiences of the day, and breathing in serenity and calm before you lie down to sleep.

MARCH

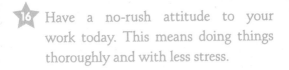

16 Have a no-rush attitude to your work today. This means doing things thoroughly and with less stress.

17 Be especially mindful of the words you use today. Speak from a place of love.

18 Take a daily routine activity, such as cleaning your teeth, and be curious and alert about yourself, noticing every sensory detail. Try it every day.

19 Keeping your life in balance means choosing to renew your energy regularly. Decide what energises you and do it today!

Today is the Spring Equinox. It is the first day of spring, a perfect time to celebrate any new beginnings that are happening in your life.

 Place a sign somewhere you can see, perhaps on a keychain, saying 'pause' and use it to help you be more mindful.

 Today become aware of your habits and how engrained they are. Try drinking your tea with sugar if you don't normally, or vice versa.

MARCH

 Spend a moment each day noticing the changes on a chosen deciduous tree. Enjoy the beauty of the tiny buds and blossom as spring progresses.

 If you find yourself dwelling on negative or anxious thoughts, bring to mind a beautiful image and allow yourself to be soothed.

 Today make a point of really listening to what people are saying, and watch you don't jump in with your view too quickly!

Your own self-realisation
is the greatest service you
can render the world.

Ramana Maharshi

Everything is phenomenal;
everything is incredible;
never treat life casually.

Abraham Joshua Heschel

28 Arrange flowers in a vase, paying attention to their beauty, texture and scent. Observe and enjoy them over the next few days.

 29 Be mindful that complaining about someone behind their back is never a positive thing to do. Combine honesty and openness with loving kindness.

 30 A mandala is a geometric pattern you can focus on to meditate. Find out more about mandalas from a good reference book: you can even create your own.

 31 Whenever you're feeling stressed, repeat this affirmation to yourself: 'All is well.'

APRIL

April Fool's Day: Laugh. If something amuses you, let the laugh escape out loud: it's a great release.

 Set your radio alarm to wake you with classical music so you begin your day with beauty and inspiration.

 Decide that from now on you will stop spreading bad news and only share good!

Your mind is your instrument. Learn to be its master and not its slave.

Remez Sasson

And sometimes the most important thing in a whole day is the rest we take between two deep breaths...

Etty Hillesum

6 While cooking today, be mindful of the actions of making a meal: washing, chopping, stirring. As you experience each process, think about the goodness the meal will give to those who eat it.

7 When shopping, send love and gratitude to the people who have produced the things that you pick up and choose to buy.

8 Swimming, riding, chi kung: any physical activity allows you to become more in touch and aware of your body. Enjoy, and be thankful!

Slow down this morning as you get dressed. Notice the textures and fabrics of your clothes and how they feel on your skin. Appreciate how many choices you have.

 Much of the time we react on a default setting. Be aware next time you are habitually responding to something without thinking, and take the space to remember that you can choose how you behave.

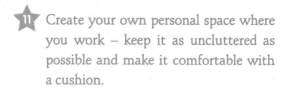

11 Create your own personal space where you work – keep it as uncluttered as possible and make it comfortable with a cushion.

12 Give yourself a mindfulness cue – something to remind you to step back into a peaceful feeling. This could be every time you hear a pigeon cooing or a clock chiming.

13 Read something positive before you go to sleep at bedtime to alleviate anxiety and replace negative thoughts with positive ones.

Eat mindfully today by chewing every mouthful twenty times. This can help you control your eating habits too.

 If you are out and about, walking the dog, observe its movements, noticing if they are harmonious or jerky and frantic. Enjoy sharing time with your pet.

 Don't be afraid to give someone you know a hug! It shows your support and affection for them.

Every breath is an
opportunity to receive and
let go. I receive love and
I let go of pain.

Brenda MacIntyre

Normally we do not so much look at things as overlook them.

Alan Watts

If you sense an argument is about to arise today, ask yourself, 'Do I want to add to disharmony or can I choose peace?'

 Focus on completing one task at a time. Research has shown that multitaskers are more likely to have high blood pressure.

 When you meet a stranger, be aware of the judgements you automatically make about them. Notice your reactions and this will lead to a less judgemental attitude.

Earth Day: Each time you empty your compost or recycling, here is a moment to be mindful of the part you play in the planet's wellbeing.

Shakespeare's Birthday: Notice today how you scan over most of your reading material. Slow down and read with your full attention, absorbing full meaning and not skipping pieces. How different does this feel from usual?

Wear some green clothing as it is the healing colour of the heart. Enjoy feeling open-hearted today!

 If you belong to a gym, while on the treadmill, meditate rather than listen to music. Make it a mental and physical workout.

 On your daily commute, whether in a vehicle or on foot, take time to really notice the surroundings you see every day.

Tread softly today, as if on a carpet of angel wings. Imagine you are surrounded by gentleness and magic.

 Carry lavender oil with you so that you can refresh yourself and your space wherever you are. The oil can be rubbed onto pulse points to aid relaxation and create a sense of calm.

Whatever the present
moment contains, accept
it as if you had chosen it.

Eckhart Tolle

But no one can get inner
peace by pouncing on it,
by vigorously willing to
have it.

Harry Emerson Fosdick

MAY

May Day: Even the shortest of walks today can be a mindful experience. Observe in detail the wildlife around you – look carefully at every leaf, bud, flower, insect and stone that catches your eye.

Whatever is happening in your life, be in acceptance, just be.

Place an image of someone inspiring where you can glance at it throughout your day. The person you have chosen can act as a reminder to be fully present.

MAY

 Embrace the smells of a new environment: focus on the delicate perfume of a flower, or the scent of newly-cut grass.

World Laughter Day (first Sunday in May): Do you remember the last time you had an uncontrollable fit of giggles? Relive the memory and laugh yourself silly again.

 If you have a pet, take extra notice of it today and enjoy each opportunity to be affectionate and caring towards it.

All our emotions are simply based on love and fear. Observe your emotions and impulses. Ask yourself, 'What do I fear here?'

 Open and close doors mindfully today – it will slow you down and perhaps be quieter!

 Tonight before you switch on the television, take a minute or two to sit and observe your breath.

 Start a new bedtime routine allowing plenty of winding-down time and a moment to be grateful for the day that's been.

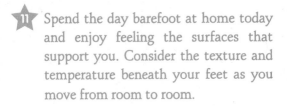

11 Spend the day barefoot at home today and enjoy feeling the surfaces that support you. Consider the texture and temperature beneath your feet as you move from room to room.

12 Take a second in between tasks to stretch your body, feeling and relaxing your muscles and joints.

13 Spend five minutes today doing nothing. Become comfortable with silence and stillness. Do this every day.

14 While waiting for your bus or train, visualise your feet planted on the earth and filling you with earth's replenishing energy.

Do you have the patience
to wait till your mud settles
and the water is clear?
Can you remain unmoving
till the right action arises
by itself?

Lao Tzu

We are what we think.
All that we are arises with
our thoughts.
With our thoughts, we
make our world.

Buddha

Incense or aromatherapy oils are lovely to burn. They clear your surroundings of sluggish air. Breathe slowly and enjoy the cleansing aromas.

 Today take time out to sit on a bench or a window seat in a cafe and people watch. Feel connected to everyone and look carefully and with compassion into their faces.

 Whether you are at home or travelling somewhere, switch off the radio or television for a while and listen to silence. You will feel calmer without all the noise of adverts, jingles and sensational news items.

Today try a walking meditation in a park or garden. Walk extra slowly, synchronising your breathing with your steps, so with each step you take a breath in or out. This connects you with your body.

 When your mind starts to flag, change your energy by moving your body; stretch, take a walk or get a drink. Be aware that you can change your energy.

 If your hands get tired from typing or any repetitive work, massage them with hand cream and be thankful for all the wonderful things hands allow you to do.

Feelings come and go like clouds in a windy sky. Conscious breathing is my anchor.

Thich Nhat Hanh

Let us be silent, that we may hear the whispers of the gods.

Ralph Waldo Emerson

If you are a parent, make sure you allow time at the end of the day to listen to your child and tell them 'I love you'.

 For every new household item that you buy, consider recycling something else.

 Hidden in the word 'listen' is the word 'silent'. Check in to your inner silence frequently today.

 How could you make your home more nurturing and calm? Spring is a great time to repaint, declutter and add beautiful plants.

Make a herbal tea. Appreciate the aroma and flavours as you make it and then spend a few tranquil moments enjoying your drink.

 While sitting at your desk, become aware of your chair and how you are sitting. Ensure your feet are placed comfortably on the ground, and your back is straight with relaxed shoulders.

 Between tasks today, rest for a moment and breathe for at least three complete breaths. This will refresh you and allow you to move smoothly on to your next job.

JUNE

⭐**1** Plan a long walk in the countryside. Turn off your mobile phone, focus on the tranquil scenery and enjoy lungfuls of fresh air.

⭐**2** Rainbows are magical. Always look out for them if it's sunny alongside the rain.

⭐**3** Imagine the Earth as seen from outer space. Visualise this image of the planet and let your heart send out love to the whole world.

JUNE

 Today, if you feel a strong emotion such as anger or shock, allow yourself to acknowledge it rather than repress it where it may fester long term and cause ill-health.

 Make the job of weeding the garden a mindful task. Imagine you are uprooting all your negative patterns and self-talk. Work methodically and with joy.

 When in a queue, stand in Mountain Pose with both feet firmly grounded, shoulders relaxed, back straight and pelvis tucked under. Breathe deeply and enjoy the wait!

The ability to simplify
means to eliminate the
unnecessary so that the
necessary may speak.

Hans Hofmann

For peace of mind we
need to resign as general
manager of the universe.

Larry Eisenberg

As you get dressed and undressed today, slow the process down and observe whether your movements are comfortable and flowing, or hasty and rushed.

10 Sit safely by fields where you can see horses, sheep or cows. Watch them and allow their slow, untroubled pace to calm you.

 Place a bowl of water strewn with flower petals in your workplace or at home. Water has many symbolic meanings – let it remind you to be at peace today.

JUNE

 Keep a notebook by your bed and record any dreams that you remember upon waking. Dreams are easily forgotten and this way you can catch them before they disappear. Sweet dreams!

 Cloud-watch. Allow the gentle movements across the sky to fill you with tranquillity and calm.

 Today, whenever you remember, whisper quietly to yourself 'I am at peace'. Let this phrase fill your being.

Let us not look back in anger or forward in fear, but around in awareness.

James Thurber

Be *passionate* about everyone and everything that enters your life.

Wayne Dyer

17 If you are feeling uncomfortable about an issue at work or at home, choose to address it this week. Take slow, deep breaths and bring your concerns to the relevant person.

 18 If you are on a long journey travelling to another part of the world, don't just be eager to arrive at your destination: allow yourself to experience new or surprising things along the way.

 19 Work slowly and deliberately on one task at a time. Keep your mind on the present, not the past or the future.

Imagine life is a movie. Watch everyone, including yourself, as though you are the audience. Relax and see how life flows before you. Don't get caught up in the drama.

 Become conscious of your breath and visualise it filling the whole of your body. A few moments of this awareness and you will feel lighter and brighter.

 As Midsummer approaches, drink in the beauty and magnificence of a sunrise or a sunset.

The point of mindfulness
is not to get rid of thought
but to learn to see
thought skilfully.

Jack Kornfield

Hey there. You've been asleep for a long time. Isn't it time to awaken?

Ajahn Chah

Have a clear-out of your garden shed or kitchen cupboards. The past is behind you – let it all go!

 Find some flowing water where you can calmly reflect – a river, the sea or ocean or even a town square fountain.

 Open all the windows around you and feel the breeze on your skin and smell the fresh air.

JUNE

 Choose a tree to observe over the days of summer, and enjoy its luscious greenery and majesty as it flourishes.

 Try something creative – draw or paint a picture, write a story about your childhood or play a piece of music.

 Today at every meal take a moment to quietly give thanks for, and bless, the food you are about to eat.

JULY

 While waiting at the bus stop or train station today, visualise you are sending out love to all your fellow travellers. It beats being grumpy!

 If you have a moment of anxiety today, place your hand on your stomach and feel the movement of your breath slowly, in and out. Feel yourself become calmer.

 Go for a swim. Imagine with each stroke you are drawing good things to you.

Blue is a healing colour for the throat and voice. To support your discussions and important talks today, wear a blue scarf or a blue crystal around your neck.

 Eat an orange mindfully – peel it slowly and enjoy the aroma. Place each segment of orange in your mouth and savour the juice. Take your time to eat this miracle of nature.

 Remember you don't need to be a super-person; one thing at a time!

 Visit a garden with flowers in bloom. Pay full attention to the scent, the colours, shapes and varieties, and enjoy their beauty.

Nowhere can man find a quieter or more untroubled retreat than in his own soul.

Marcus Aurelius

If you want others to
be happy, practise
compassion.
If you want to be happy,
practise compassion.

The Dalai Lama

JULY

 Be aware of phrases you often repeat throughout the day – some of these may be part of a negative pattern. Be kinder to yourself.

 Bring your attention to the movement of your feet whenever you travel up and down stairs. It will help you to slow down.

 Carry a single leaf or feather with you today and spend frequent moments observing it. Allow its beauty to uplift and heal you.

 Today make a conscious effort to reduce your talking and see how silence can hold you in a calm space.

JULY

 If the grass needs cutting this week, use this chore as an opportunity to be fully mindful. Bring your scattered thoughts back to the task whenever they wander.

 Enjoy your sense of smell today – rain-drenched earth, freshly-baked bread, fresh fruit or barbecue smoke.

 Notice birds – flying outside your window, paddling on a pond, chattering in the shrubs or feeding on the ground. Wildlife can make you smile and inspire your sense of wonder.

17 This morning, notice things you are thankful for – a hot shower, clean clothes and fresh food. Make gratitude a daily practice.

18 Find a few minutes in your morning routine to sit quietly and greet the day ahead, before rushing into day-to-day activities.

19 Before you settle to sleep, send out loving thoughts to those close to you, those you work with, your community, the peoples of the world and lastly to yourself.

Try to find a wide horizon from a hilltop and let your eyes lose focus into the distance. The lack of sharp focus is very calming.

 When did you last sing joyously? Sing like a child, without care or inhibition.

 When you return from a holiday abroad, it's great to have the memories, but don't just daydream about when your next trip away will be. Be present in your daily life and enjoy the new perspective some time away can bring.

God, give us grace to accept
with serenity the things that
cannot be changed,
Courage to change the things
which should be changed,
and the Wisdom to distinguish
the one from the other.

Reinhold Niebuhr

When you lack understanding and you are unable to control your mind, your senses do not obey you, just as unruly horses do not obey a charioteer.

The Upanishads

25 Have fun this weekend by organising an activity you haven't done for a while. It's important to balance work and play.

 26 Take a day to discover something new in the place where you live.

 27 Try running, as it gives you time to focus on your body and breathing as well as being great exercise.

 28 Plan a picnic with a friend and enjoy their company in a beautiful location away from life's stresses.

Take extra care of your appearance and feel good as you walk out the door.

 Today consider the concept of non-attachment. It means being flexible and not clinging to a fixed idea. Things don't always happen the way you expect them to.

 Smile at people you pass.

AUGUST

1 Get up ten to twenty minutes earlier than usual so that you are not rushed in the morning. Make this your daily routine.

2 After a swim, take time to float in the water and focus on the feeling of drifting. Empty your tension into the water.

3 Walking in nature is the most replenishing thing you can do – don't chatter endlessly with a friend, instead walk side by side in silence. Experience all the sights, smells and sounds around you.

AUGUST

 Watch fish in a pond or an aquarium. This very peaceful activity of focusing on their serene movements will help you to feel calm.

 As you prepare your meal tonight stop to notice every culinary aroma that arises while you chop, weigh, steam, fry and serve. Allow each new aroma to awaken your sense of smell.

World Meditation Day takes place on the first Sunday of every month. Breathe deeply and go with the flow.

Move outside the tangle
of fear-thinking. Live
in silence.

Rumi

Nature does not hurry, yet everything is accomplished.

Lao Tzu

9 If you are travelling to new destinations this month be open and interested in unfamiliar customs and cultures.

 10 Focus on an object from nature such as a flower or a seashell. See its beauty and intricacy, and place all other thoughts to one side while you marvel at the detail of this natural object.

 11 When you are out and about today, notice the street busker or charity collector. Stop to exchange money and a few words.

Imagine that within your heart you carry around a lighted candle. See others too, with their flames glowing. Appreciate the light in everyone!

International Left-Handers Day: Eat with chopsticks or eat with your non-dominant hand – if it's something you are not used to then this concentrates the mind wonderfully on the eating process.

 Remember you don't always have to say yes. Open up some space in your life by saying 'no!'

15 Make your bed each morning purposefully so you create a calm transition from bedroom and sleep to the outside world and the rest of your day.

16 Today while you drive, let cars speed past you, even cut you up. Send their drivers good wishes, 'May you be well, may you be happy.'

17 If you are doing some gardening this weekend focus on the physical experience and be open to all your senses. Observe how your mind wants to rush off to other things.

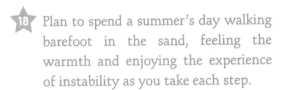

18 Plan to spend a summer's day walking barefoot in the sand, feeling the warmth and enjoying the experience of instability as you take each step.

19 Spend a minute before you go to sleep tonight counting your blessings – saying thank you for all the good things from your day.

20 While washing up today, do this chore mindfully, noticing every rainbow bubble, the warm water and the shining dishes.

My first responsibility is to myself, to treat myself with love and compassion.

Dr Brenda Davies

Peace comes from within. Do not seek it without.

Buddha

If you feel stressed today place your hand over your heart area. Feel the warmth and know that you are loved.

 Plan a mindful weekend without clocks or watches. Listen to your body instead – you choose when to get up, when to eat, what tasks you feel like doing and the length of time you spend on them.

 A cycle ride in the countryside gives you the chance to connect with nature. Plan a day out and keep it relaxed and fun.

Plan a growing project, even if it is just a window box. Plant the seeds, water them and tend your new living thing with mindfulness and love.

 Even when walking through a bustling city turn your eye to details – chimneys, rooftops, windows and the abundant variety of architectural features.

 Notice patterns today – symmetry, circles, spirals, parallel lines, pairs and repetition. Each time allow your gaze to stay a moment longer in wonder.

29 If you feel impatient at any time today, be curious about the thoughts that occur. Allow yourself to be still and count slowly to three.

 30 Some people and activities can drain your energy. When this happens, remember to be centred and rooted firmly like a tree.

 31 If you are hanging out washing to dry, take your time with every item of clothing and notice how much of a pleasure slowing down can be.

SEPTEMBER

 Today, inside and out, notice the sunlight. It can stream in through your window or dazzle you from between the clouds. Absorb it and luxuriate in its warmth.

 When you feel tension, become aware of your body. Imagine you are dropping further into your legs and feet to ground yourself. Breathe in and out, thinking love and peace.

 Go on a 'sensing' walk where you notice any object that attracts you. Bring into sharp focus your senses of sight, sound, smell, touch and taste.

True solitude is a din of
birdsong, seething leaves,
whirling colours, or a
clamour of tracks in
the snow.

Edward Hoagland

And joy is everywhere;
It is in the earth's green
covering of grass;
In the blue serenity of
the sky...

Rabindranath Tagore

6 As you prepare a meal today pay attention to your sense of sound. To hold your mind to that task say to yourself 'sound'. You may be amazed at how much your ears are hearing.

7 Whisper to yourself 'thank you' for all the things you notice today that make life better, are amazing, are beautiful or which make you smile.

8 Notice when you are judging things as good or bad. Pause. Tell yourself there doesn't need to be good or bad: life happens. Feel light and free.

When you read an email, do something with it; respond, delete or archive. Don't become swamped.

 Create a display with objects that are meaningful, a candle and a picture of an inspiring person. Sit by this space for a few quiet moments when you can, or let it remind you to be peaceful as you pass by.

 A problem arises at work. Imagine you are close to the end of your life and you look at this problem before you. Does it seem so important now?

Mindfulness Day: When our minds are engulfed with stories of our past or future, we are missing the experience of the moment. Today, keep remembering the moments you are in.

 Drink up! Today don't allow cups of tea to sit undrunk on your desk. Give yourself a moment to relax and enjoy your cuppa.

 Take a mindful moment today to look out of the window and drink in the changing scenery.

Listen to your body – it is continually communicating to you, and by paying attention to headaches, stiff shoulders, a 'funny' tummy or itchy skin, we can sense problems and stop them becoming worse.

 For decision-making, you need to drop below the level of noise and chatter in your mind to the quiet, still space of your heart where you will hear your true voice – the one to listen to.

 Observe the water flowing from the tap as you fill the sink or bathtub: notice its pure beauty and its sound while gushing down for you to use.

This moment is all there is.

Rumi

Finding solitude in the
concrete jungle is powerful
and peaceful.

Mike Dolan

While sitting on the tube, train or bus, become aware of fellow passengers and send loving thoughts to them: 'I send you love, and hope all goes well for you today.'

International Day of Peace: Find a poem or prayer that has peace as its message. Write it out and attach it somewhere like your fridge. Read it whenever you wish to be inspired, especially today.

SEPTEMBER

Autumn Equinox: Look out for the huge and wonderful Harvest Moon. Drink in its beauty.

 If you get the chance with your own or a friend's toddler, see the world from their viewpoint with wonder and excitement: jump in puddles, pick up sticks, look closely at bugs or finger-paint together.

 Today allow yourself to take a different route home from work. While not on 'autopilot' you see your surroundings in a new way.

If you are having a good tidy-up today, remember we arrived here with nothing and we take nothing when we go.

 Go and harvest some fruit – blackberries, apples or pears. Be present to the process and relish the sharp flavours and deep colours of your freshly-picked fruit.

 Today's affirmation for you to repeat silently in your mind whenever you remember is 'slow down'.

Just for today, listen more and talk less.

 On waking today, decide that you will look for the secret goodness in three people you deal with. Open your heart as you speak with them and notice how this intention affects things.

 Organise a small surprise for your children, your partner or a friend that will make them happy. The benefit is that you feel happier too.

OCTOBER

 There's never a day when it's not good to be thankful for the hot, plentiful water that provides your shower or bath. It's worth reminding yourself throughout the day: Thank you. I am truly blessed.

 While waiting for the kettle to boil, take the opportunity to breathe more deeply and look out of the window at the expanse of sky above.

If you are feeling overwhelmed, close your eyes and visualise ascending some steps. With every breath take a step upwards, out of the dark confusion, until you feel lighter at the top of the staircase.

 Regard cleaning the bathroom as a positive exercise which can allow you to alleviate stress and even tone your muscles.

The greatest step towards a life of simplicity is to learn to let go.

Steve Maraboli

O Nobly Born, remember
your own loving heart.
Trust it, honour it, follow it.
It will bring you peace.

Buddha

To distinguish between your work and your leisure, use your journey home to bring your mindful attention to your breath. Let go of the activities and worries of the working day and arrive home relaxed.

 All words contain energy and vibration; therefore, transform your inner critic to a voice of kindness and love.

 Enjoy the clouds as they scud across the sky – everything is in a constant process of change.

Visualise a flower of your choice across a person's heart. Visualise your own flower too. Imagine the petals opening so you can communicate in a loving manner.

 Keep in touch with friends and family, even if it's a quick email or a postcard.

 Today choose a slow activity for you to relax and unwind. Try a boat ride, a spa visit or a massage.

13 Place wind chimes outside your window at work or home. When you hear them chime, take a deeper, slower breath towards peace and calm.

 14 'Calm abiding' is a mindfulness term that you could recite to yourself today. Carry the notion around with you.

 15 Rose quartz is the crystal of love. Keep a piece of this crystal where you will see it, to remind yourself that you are loved, or give one to someone else so they can be reminded too.

Notice the turning of the leaves of your chosen deciduous tree. Allow it to remind you that all things change and move on.

 Reduce your information consumption. Cancel subscriptions for magazines you barely have time to read and unsubscribe from catalogues and junk mail.

 When you look in the mirror today say, 'Thank you. This is who I am.'

Having a wider heart and mind is more important than having a larger house.

Venerable Cheng Yen

... there is nothing either good or bad, but thinking makes it so...

William Shakespeare, *Hamlet*

Apple Day: Eat an apple slowly with appreciation for its taste, smell and texture. Celebrate Apple Day by baking an apple pie and sharing its deliciousness with others.

 Plan to have a luxurious bath this evening, being mindful of all your senses. Enjoy the warm water, the bath oils, scented candles, fluffy towels and relaxing music.

 Repeat these words as frequently as you can today: 'Let it be.' Notice how it allows you to be accepting of what happens.

Take a moment at lunchtime to escape work's bustle and enjoy your midday meal.

 When you start a task today, finish it completely. Focus on one thing at a time.

 While queuing today, do not be distracted by looking at your watch or becoming anxious. Instead enjoy the pause in life as you wait, and allow energy to flow around your body.

Choose to learn how to play a musical instrument. It focuses your mind and can lead to a lot of enjoyment.

 If your mind won't slow down, observe and identify your emotions without having to resolve them. 'I am feeling scared,' 'I am worried,' 'I feel angry,' etc.

 Experience nature by going out and walking amongst fallen leaves. Focus on their colour, their texture and the sound as you swoosh through them. Delight in the smell of autumn.

30 Whenever your mind strays from a task – stop. With one hand touch your forefinger and thumb together for a complete breath. Continue your task and see how your experience changes.

Halloween: Find a new recipe for cooking pumpkin or squash. Enjoy the sense of cooking something different and sharing it with friends.

NOVEMBER

1 Animals don't worry about what happened yesterday or what they will be doing tonight. So just for today, be like a cat!

2 Early morning frosts and mist can transform the world around you. Take a moment to admire the beauty that cold temperatures have created.

3 Today frequently remind yourself with this gentle phrase, 'I am at peace.'

NOVEMBER

 4 Gaze into a fire and allow the flames to mesmerise and calm you.

 5 Bonfire Night: Enjoy being fully present as you participate with friends in celebrating with fireworks and food.

 6 If you are a passenger today, appreciate and enjoy the ever-changing passing scenery.

 7 Buy yourself a daylight lamp which simulates natural daylight, reduces eye strain and has a warm and nourishing feel.

Learn to get in touch with the silence within yourself and know that everything in this life has a purpose.

Elisabeth Kübler-Ross

Patience, then, is really
another word for letting go
of fear and worry.

Doreen Virtue

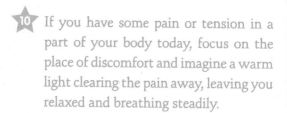

10 If you have some pain or tension in a part of your body today, focus on the place of discomfort and imagine a warm light clearing the pain away, leaving you relaxed and breathing steadily.

11 Attune your ears to listen for the sounds of night-time as you settle to sleep. Be fully present with all noises, outside and in.

12 Try a new skill today. The experience of learning brings you fully into the present.

Be aware next time you are about to gossip – be mindful of the words you share.

 Make a habit of looking out of your window at night. Then you won't miss those moments when the sky is full of stars or a full moon takes your breath away.

 Listen to a piece of classical music today in complete stillness and pay undivided attention to it. Afterwards notice how much calmer you feel.

Everything you do can be
done better from a place
of relaxation.

Stephen C. Paul

I never came upon any of my discoveries through the process of rational thinking.

Albert Einstein

If you ride a bicycle or motorbike, you will be in direct contact with your environment. Be mindful of all around you is a life-saving attitude.

 Schedule space for in between tasks. You may then find that you don't need to rush or do more than one thing at a time.

 Learn this phrase and recite it to yourself wherever you walk: 'May I walk with peace and serenity in my heart as my feet kiss the earth with gratitude.'

Find out where you can go locally to join in with chanting or a scratch choir. Open your heart and voice to making sound.

 Count to ten when you feel like saying something to a loved one that is better left unsaid. Find ways of sharing how you feel rather than making accusations.

 Organise tasks you must do according to how much energy you have — perhaps tackle more demanding jobs in the morning when your energy reserves are high.

Visit an art exhibition this week and spend time looking with care at the paintings and sculptures. Notice how each piece evokes a feeling in you.

 Take time to listen to a river or the sea – just listen.

 Be a compassionate friend to yourself by expressing loving kindness in all that you do. Even when you make mistakes, say this reminder, 'It's OK.'

 In a storm listen to the wind and rain; notice the sounds and accept how they make you feel.

NOVEMBER

 Think about experiences that deplete your energy or lead to a passive state, and reduce them. This could be television, internet surfing, computer games or lying in bed too long.

 Set a timer to allow yourself to sit and completely focus on your breath for one minute. Do nothing else, and simply allow all thoughts to arise without getting involved in them.

 Make time for your friends and be open to them sharing their thoughts with you. True friendships are about listening and speaking from the heart.

DECEMBER

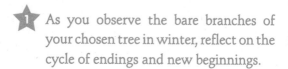 As you observe the bare branches of your chosen tree in winter, reflect on the cycle of endings and new beginnings.

Notice how you may be reacting to stress – perhaps drinking more alcohol or caffeine, eating too little or too much, or disconnecting with your partner. Choose a different response such as exercise, meditating or talking about it.

When you walk in through your front door, stop and take a deep breath. I am home. I am safe.

DECEMBER

 Make your own greetings cards or create your own poem for the season, so that your friends and family receive something loving and unique from you.

 Allow yourself plenty of rest over the busy festive season when there may be more demands on your time.

 Visit a food market at home or abroad and allow your senses to enjoy every vibrant aspect around you.

 Go through the day as if you were an undercover Dalai Lama. See the best in everyone!

We too should make
ourselves empty, that the
great soul of the universe
may fill us with its breath.

Laurence Binyon

... anxiety does not empty tomorrow of its sorrows, but only empties today of its strength.

Charles H. Spurgeon

10 Think about addressing imbalances in your day. Perhaps you need more physical activity away from the computer, more time to pursue your own interests, or more quality time with children and family.

11 Don't let yourself get overwhelmed by a problem. Take one small step at a time and never be afraid to ask for help.

12 Buy a CD of guided meditations. Listen to it regularly to help you build a meditation routine. Notice how this benefits your being mindful in daily life.

DECEMBER

13 When you take a mindful walk it is about the journey and not the destination. Focus on the walk!

14 When family tensions are feeling too intense, imagine zooming out to the solar system and view everyone as tiny specks.

15 Take notice of the shop assistant who serves you – even a smile may cheer them up.

16 When you share Christmas greetings, say them with meaning and love.

Nothing is worth more than this day.

Johann Wolfgang von Goethe

DECEMBER

 At a party, take a moment to step back from the talking and dancing, and experience the sounds that wash around you as a kind of music.

 Find a recipe to make bird cake or fat balls. Place them outside where you can stop at moments in the day to observe and appreciate your bird visitors.

 For mindfulness tips to become stored in your long-term memory, they need to be done at least four times. Today choose one of your favourite tips from the year and use it regularly.

We have more possibilities available in each moment than we realise.

Thich Nhat Hanh

When walking, walk.
When eating, eat.

Zen proverb

DECEMBER

 The holiday season can bring a sharp reminder that we are truly blessed in our comfortable lives. Allow yourself to feel gratitude and share what you can with those less fortunate.

 During the days of deepest winter be aware that this is a time for regeneration, for relaxing and cocooning yourself in quiet and reflective moments.

Winter Solstice: In the heart of midwinter we can be appreciative of our warm cosy homes and all the comforts that we have.

DECEMBER

 22 Enjoy the traditions of the season as they give you the opportunity to build happy memories with family and friends.

 23 Notice as anxiety builds up you may unconsciously hold your breath. Stop and allow your breathing to become slower and deeper before you continue on your way.

 24 The festive season involves a wealth of wonderful aromas. Open up your sense of smell and memory with roasting chestnuts, pine trees, mulled wine and gingerbread!

Christmas Day: If you have friends or family coming round to eat today, keep it simple; don't worry about impressing them. Be mindful of what is truly important – friendship and sharing food.

Boxing Day: Use family gatherings to practise mindful listening. Any family member will appreciate your complete attention and both of you benefit from this exchange.

While on a shopping trip today be aware of all the people you pass by. Look into their faces and send out loving thoughts to every one of them.